Does your Palate Need Cleansing?

BONITA WOMACK

Copyright © 2023 Bonita Womack

All rights reserved. This publication may not be reproduced in any form without permission in writing from the publisher. Unauthorized reproduction of any part of this work is illegal and is punishable by law.

Scripture references are used with permission from Zondervan via Biblegateway.com

ISBN 978-1-950861-79-8

PRINTED IN THE UNITED STATES OF AMERICA

His Glory Creations Publishing, LLC
Wendell, North Carolina

ACKNOWLEDGMENTS

To my heavenly Father, I would like to thank You for life, health, strength, and for speaking to me through the Holy Spirit concerning my palate. Thank You for changing my life.

I would like to acknowledge my late mom and stepfather, Catherine and Willie Butler, who instilled so much into me and pushed me to be all God called me to be.

I would like to acknowledge my late husband, Bobby Womack Sr. It was after watching him go through his illness that I realized I needed a palate cleansing-the palate of my heart and my mind needed cleaning. I'm eternally grateful for all his encouragement and his desire to see me be my best self.

To my siblings, thank you for your continuous support. I love each of you dearly.

To my beautiful goddaughters, handsome godsons, spiritual sons and daughters, I love you all and thank you for everything that you bring into my life. I also would like to acknowledge my three grandchildren who have been a blessing to me.

A special thank you to my goddaughter, Monisha Parker, for her unending willingness to assist in this project. Thank you from the bottom of my heart for helping to give shape to this book.

To my Pastors, Apostle Phillip Anthony Walker, Co-Pastor Vickie Walker, and Assistant Pastor Nettie Kershaw of Mount Pleasant Worship and Outreach Center Church, you have been my covering for several years and I thank God for you. You have been there for me for so many things. Thank you for your excellent leadership. I've not always done everything that you taught or preached. You never gave up on me. Thank you for pushing me to be the best that I can be, continuously encouraging me along the way and for investing in my life. Many thanks and gratitude to the Mt. Pleasant Worship and Outreach Center Church family for your encouragement and support. I love you all dearly.

To my spiritual Mother, Apostle Shirley R. Brown, thank you for your continuous love and support in ministry and in my personal life. You have been a huge blessing in my life, and I love you dearly.

I would like to acknowledge my late spiritual father, Pastor John W. Highsmith Sr. He was such a blessing in my life, and I thank God for the time I spent with him. Thank you to his family who welcome and accept me as one of their own.

I would like to thank the Reed family for all of your love and support and accepting me into the family.

To the Womack family, thank you for your love and support over the years.

Lastly, thank you to the many others whom I cannot yet begin to name. God has blessed me through your support.

Contents

Introduction 1

Chapter 1 – Foretaste 3

Chapter 2 – Bittersweet 11

Chapter 3 – A Bad Taste in My Mouth 17

Chapter 4 – Sweet 25

Chapter 5 – Unsavory 29

Chapter 6 – Salty 35

Chapter 7 – Distasteful 41

Chapter 8 – Unappetizing 47

Chapter 9 – Refreshment 53

Chapter 10 – Leftovers for Your Takeout 61

About the Author 63

Introduction

Life experiences have a way of leaving a lingering aftertaste in our mouth, whether it's bitter or sweet, savory, or unsavory. I've learned through the years that it takes God, who is our palate cleanser, to help us digest life experiences and the toll it takes on our life. In life, we go through many things. Sometimes those things have a way of scarring us. Apostle Paul tells us, "Therefore, if anyone cleanses himself from these things [which are dishonorable-disobedient, sinful], he will be a vessel for honor, sanctified [set apart for a special purpose and], useful to the Master, prepared for every good work" (2 Timothy 2:2, AMP).

CHAPTER 1

Foretaste

According to Freedictionary.com, foretaste is defined as "a slight and partial experience, knowledge, or taste of something to come in the future."

One February morning, in the early part of 2020, I got up, and my husband was in bed sleeping. I was in the bathroom doing my hair, and the Lord spoke to me. He told me to go over to look at my husband. When I looked down at Bobby, I could tell he was sick. God showed me sickness in his body. I had never seen this on anyone before. As I continued to prepare for the day, God instructed me a second time to go look at my husband.

This time, I walked over and saw him lying there as if he was a dead person. I could not believe what I was seeing. I was frightened, baffled, and confused. I immediately left his bedside, closed the bedroom door, and walked into the kitchen. I said to God, "What is this? What are you showing me?" There was complete silence. He said nothing. The vision of him lying in bed played over and over in my head all morning and was engrained in my brain.

When he got up, I insisted that he see his doctor to see if they could determine what was wrong with him. For days, he had a persistent cough and experienced a higher body temperature than usual. He expressed to me that something was wrong with him, and he was uncomfortably hot.

He thought something was wrong with our mattress. I knew he was going through something in his body, but I didn't know what it was, and I didn't know how to help him. I asked him several times to go to the doctor. I was nervous and scared but could not share what God had just revealed to me with anyone. I knew that something was going on with my husband and wanted him to be seen immediately.

As you know, sometimes when we tell our spouses something, they oftentimes don't listen. My husband refused to go to the doctor and kept taking cold medicine. He purchased various ones because he felt like he had a cold. He was coughing and experiencing shortness of breath, but he didn't tell me at the time. I continued to encourage him to see a doctor. Of course, he didn't go. I was concerned, but I kept the matter in prayer.

In March, he finally admitted he was having shortness of breath, and he went to the VA Hospital. When he arrived, they kept him because he had fluid around his lungs. He remained in the hospital for a week because they wanted to make sure he didn't have tuberculosis, pneumonia or COVID. While there, they also ran tests to check for cancer.

Three liters of fluid were removed from around his lungs. The medical staff ruled out tuberculosis, pneumonia, and COVID. They eventually sent him home. It would be weeks later before the results of the cancer screening would be available. In the meantime, he again began to experience shortness of breath. He felt the fluid in his lungs may be returning. Finally, after several more weeks, we were informed that no cancer had been detected. I was so relieved. Even though I was elated with this news, I could not help thinking about what God had previously shown me about my husband. At this point, I was thankful to God because I thought removing the fluid from his lungs would save his life.

He pressed on even though he was not feeling one hundred percent. We continued to seek medical care because he was still experiencing discomfort. It was in May 2020, two months after his initial hospital visit, that my husband received a diagnosis of non-carcinoma lung cancer. Being told there was no cancer detected in March, then being told his body was riddled with cancer in May, sent me into a whirlwind of emotions.

You can't imagine the shock we experienced from this new diagnosis! Weeks earlier, the diagnosis was no cancer! Unfortunately, the cancer, which started in his lungs, had spread throughout his body, including his brain. When your body tells you something is not right, please listen. I didn't know how to receive that information.

As a woman of God and a prayer warrior, I really didn't know what to do except pray. I didn't know what God was preparing me for or what was about to happen. It felt like an out-of-body experience. I could see everything being played out in front of me, and there was nothing I could do. This was a difficult place for me. As I began to ask people to pray for him, the only thing I could say was to pray because God can do anything but fail! I believed God, and I knew He could turn anything around. Even though He showed me what He showed me, we know that we can pray. I prayed and asked friends and several prayer ministries to pray with me.

My prayer partners, Bridget Nelson Hodge and Judy Reed, prayed with me almost daily for this situation to turn around. We held early morning prayer sessions. These prayer warriors and our families stood by us as we walked through this storm. Several members of Bobby's family came to pray with us. Many traveled far and near, coming from different parts of the country to join in prayer. So many people interceded with us and for us during this time. Even though there were many bombarding Heaven, I had to pray for myself and keep myself encouraged.

My husband and I were going to walk a painful and difficult journey over the next three months. He would eventually succumb to cancer in August of 2020, which left me with many emotional wounds that needed to be healed. That was not the end of my story, and it does not have to be the end of yours either.

Even though our marital journey would end, the next phase of my life was before me with so many new experiences to savor. Was I ready for this next phase? I thought I was, however, God had other plans.

One Word

In February 2021, God spoke one word to me through the Holy Spirit, and that word was *palate*. I walked around repeating it in my mind and talking to the Lord saying, "I know what the word means, but what are You saying to me?" I knew the meaning of *palate*, but wasn't sure of what He was speaking to me. The next day I heard the Lord crystal clearly telling me that the palate of my heart and mind needed cleansing.

This led to God vastly expanding the scope and view of my life. There were so many things that came to my mind as I pondered the word *palate*. I began to see things and feel things I was apparently not fully conscious of before. I was experiencing or *tasting* things that affected my spirit and not necessarily in a positive manner.

What is a Palate Cleanser?

I researched this phrase. A palate cleanser is a neutral-flavored food or beverage that is used to remove food residue from your tongue to allow you to accurately assess a new flavor. It ultimately prepares you for the next course. Like any cleanser, once the lingering flavors of your previous course have been removed, you are able to enjoy the next course with a *fresh perspective*. When your palate is cleansed, it improves digestion and can stimulate your appetite. Stimulating your appetite is one point that stood out to me.

If a palate cleanser helps to improve your digestion, it can assist in helping your system flow properly, which in turn can improve one's state of being. Without proper flow, you could be overweight, miserable, depressed, filled with anxiety, bitterness or hate, blinded, stuck in a season, and even physically sick.

Another quality of the palate cleanser is that it removes any lingering aftertaste. I had a lot of life's lingering aftertastes, which I was not aware of until God revealed it to me.

In case you haven't figured it out already, I did not write an entire book about how to prepare for your next meal course. However, I did want to share what God revealed to me about the importance of cleansing your *spiritual palate*.

The following scriptures state it best, "So here's what I want you to do, God helping you: Take your everyday, ordinary life—your sleeping, eating, going-to-work, and walking-around life—and place it before God as an offering. Embracing what God does for you is the best thing you can do for him. Don't become so well-adjusted to your culture that you fit into it without even thinking. Instead, fix your attention on God. You'll be changed from the inside out. Readily recognize what he wants from you and quickly respond to it. Unlike the culture around you, always dragging you down to its level of immaturity, God brings the best out of you, develops well-formed maturity in you" (Romans 12:1-2, MSG).

There were so many times when I conformed to the culture. I needed God to change my mindset because I had some *stinking thinking*. I needed God to cleanse my palate.

My thinking was warped because of the things I experienced, many of which were not pleasing to me or God. I didn't realize some of the things I endured during my husband's sickness and transition had changed my view. I needed a mind and heart change. Not a mind or heart change, but both.

This is where my palate cleansing began. God cleansed the palate of my mind, which led to a heart change. When the palate of our mind is cleansed, the necessary heart change will occur, which will allow us to properly savor His abundant life. This has been the most rewarding change in my entire life.

We all know how the taste of one thing can affect the flavor of the next. It's imperative that our palates are frequently cleansed, so we can fully enjoy our next level from a fresh perspective without the lingering residue of things we consumed from the past.

Palate cleansers are often used between tasting wine, cheese, or other strong flavors. Only after your palate is cleansed can you savor your food again. You can't assess new flavors unless you remove the old residue. That was one of my problems. The residue from past relationships, trials, and experiences in my life had caused me to have a dirty palate. Therefore, I was unable to assess anything new. Past feelings, thoughts, and residue were hindering me from assessing anything new.

To cleanse my palate, I realized I had to start eliminating some of the things that caused my palate to be dirty. Unfortunately, it was mostly the *stinking thinking* in my mind. I needed to have a renewed mind. The only way I knew to do this was with God's help and guidance. Everybody's journey is not going to be the same.

I listened to the Holy Spirit and was obedient to His promptings and allowed Him to begin the cleansing process. Despite having experienced much in life, I now feel the true freedom of living life to the fullest. God has changed my mindset on a lot of things because He made me aware of my dirty palate.

As you read this book about my journey, you may find this applies to your life as it did mine. I wanted to share my journey over the following pages of how God cleansed my palate. It has changed my life. God reminded me and revealed to me the areas that needed cleansing in my life. I was surprised at some of the things He said to me.

Again, our palates can get dirty from various things that have occurred in our lives and have caused us pain, those things that have made us act in a manner that's not pleasing to God. We are often stuck on old things and consistently do the same things we've always done, yet we expect different results.

According to Albert Einstein, "Insanity is doing the same thing over and over and expecting different results." Once you begin to cleanse that residue by allowing God to get rid of some of the old, you can expand your palate and learn to savor the new. As I allow God to cleanse my palate, I am now being more adventurous. I am experiencing life and being present in the experience.

There were many things that caused my palate to be dirty, as you will see throughout this book. Even though it has been a process, God is not through with me yet, I can see and feel Him removing many of the residues that have hindered me.

CHAPTER 2

Bittersweet

According to the Merriam-Webster Dictionary, bittersweet is defined as "being at once bitter and sweet; especially, pleasant but including or marked by elements of suffering or regret. Bittersweet memories."

One bittersweet memory was revealed to me that I had residue from past relationships that needed to be cleaned. For example, Bobby and I would sometimes fuss about him not keeping my car clean. He would say, "I will clean your car if you ride to the car wash with me." In past relationships, my companions always cleaned my car without me having to be present. I was accustomed to someone else keeping the car clean.

I know this was petty, but it was an issue for me. Sometimes the little things can create big problems. My husband wanted to create a new experience with me, but the residue from the past in this area prevented me from embracing anything different.

Your palate can also become dirty, not only from things you do, but because of what others do to you. For example, in a previous relationship, you may have experienced marital infidelity. Because of that hurt, trust issues developed. Most people won't open themselves up to that pain anymore. Some people refuse to enter another serious relationship, and those who do sometimes bring trust issues with them. They start a new relationship with crippling, bittersweet memories.

As my pastor, Apostle Phillip Walker, stated, "Everybody has stuff. However, it is how we think about our stuff that determines our circumstances and the emotions behind our thoughts. The things happening to you are not the feelings. It is how you think about what is happening to you that creates the feelings. For example, when someone hurts our feelings, they only hurt us one time. Each time we think about the situation, we reinjure ourselves again. For example, suppose someone stabs our heart with a whetted insult that penetrates like a knife. We can remove the knife yet reinjure ourselves additional times by replaying the situation repeatedly in our minds. Therefore, we are inflicting needless pain. They only stabbed us once; we hurt ourselves the other 99 times. It is not just your emotions that are painful. It is your thoughts that are painful. We cannot allow our circumstances to overpower our thoughts."

When we allow our circumstances to overpower our thoughts, it affects our palate. However, if you allow God to cleanse your palate, you are more apt to be open-minded in life experiences. You can begin to trust again and therefore love again. Your observation, awareness, and perception all become clearer. You become acquainted or reacquainted with so many things you missed before.

This is not to say that you will never be hurt again or experience pain; however, you will be able to see things from a different perspective and handle them in a different manner.

As your palate is being cleansed from bittersweet memories, you suddenly begin to have the desire to experience new things. These may be things you would have never thought of doing before.

After giving my life to the Lord, I attended Bible College, as I felt the Lord calling me to minister the gospel. I also completed a leadership certification course at the University of Notre Dame to enhance my personal and professional growth. I never would have enrolled in a degree program with the mindset I previously had.

I always told people I was blessed to get out of high school. School and test-taking have always been a challenge for me. I was so grateful I graduated before end-of-school exit exams were a requirement. Once I graduated, I was adamant about not seeking higher education. I had convinced myself that was something I could not accomplish.

At the beginning of 2021, I could see and feel the cleansing process taking place. I remembered when God spoke to me concerning cleansing my palate. The first thing that came to my mind was the following verses, "Create in me a clean heart, O God; and renew the right spirit within me, oh Lord" (Psalm 51:10 KJV).

Another scripture in my spirit read, "I will sprinkle clean water on you and ye shall be clean from all your uncleanliness, and from all your idols I will cleanse you and I will give you a new heart and a new spirit and I will put within you and I will remove the heart of stone from your flesh and give you a heart of flesh and I will put my Spirit within you and cause you to walk in my statutes and be careful to obey my rules" (Ezekiel 36:25-27, ESV).

When I thought about those Scriptures, I said to the Lord, "I need a heart that's sensitive to Your touch. Just like I heard You say my palate needed cleansing, and I began to respond to that, I now need a clean heart. I need a clean heart to hear You and to do those things You are telling me to do during this season in my life." I give God glory that I listened to Him.

I understand exactly what Jeremiah was saying, "The heart is deceitful above all things, and desperately sick; who can understand it? I the Lord search the heart and test the mind, to give every man according to his ways, according to the fruit of his deeds" (Jeremiah 17:9-10, ESV). I responded, "Help me Lord Jesus!"

Apostle Peter stated, "Having purified your souls by your obedience to the truth for a sincere brotherly love, love one another earnestly from a pure heart" (1 Peter 1:22, ESV). I realized I cannot love from a pure heart if my palate is dirty. Scripture states, "Let the words of my mouth and the meditation of my heart be acceptable in Your sight oh Lord, my Rock and my Redeemer." I repeated this again to God, "Lord let the words of my mouth and the meditation of my heart be acceptable in Your sight, oh Lord, my Rock and my Redeemer" (Psalm 19:14, ESV). I have said many things I should not have said; I have done things I should not have done, but I thank God for His grace and mercy that has kept me.

Self-Reflection:

When the palate of our mind is cleansed, the necessary heart change will occur, which will allow us to properly savor His abundant life.

1. Do you have a bittersweet palate? If so, what has caused your palate to become bittersweet?

_____

_____

_____

_____

_____

_____

_____

_____

2. What can you do to make it sweeter?

3. What Scripture is God speaking to you right now?

Scripture References:

Psalm 51:10
Ezekiel 36:25-27
Jeremiah 17:9-10
1 Peter 1:22
Psalm 19:14

CHAPTER 3

A Bad Taste in My Mouth

Merriam-Webster Dictionary states "a bad taste in someone's mouth is to make someone feel bad or disgusted."

We have all heard someone say an experience or person left *a bad taste* in their mouth. This has little to nothing to do with the sense of taste and everything to do with the familiarity of an unpleasant feeling, a feeling we often thought we had forgotten until it comes up again. All of a sudden, you're back in that place, that knot in your throat, the uneasiness in your stomach, or the hair standing on your neck. We are all familiar with that *taste*.

I have vivid memories of an incident that I experienced with my husband before his death. This was an incident that nearly derailed our marriage. During my palate cleansing journey, I was reminded of this incident that left a really bad taste in my mouth. One night while minding my business, I discovered some information that really upset me. This information made me both heartbroken and angry. It reminded me of something I went through in the past. I found myself in a place where I wanted to lash out and get out of character. *The Bo-Nita* wanted to show up, and that is someone nobody wants to tangle with. When I'm upset, if I don't calm down quickly, I will make a mess. What I saw threw me into a rage and *Bo-Nita* showed up (the old Bonita). Those of you who know me know exactly what I mean.

We have all had experiences which have left a lingering bad taste in our mouths. We continually experience the aftertaste from the unpleasant each time we reflect on what occurred.

Thank God for the new Bonita. Instead of giving into my flesh (the do-it-yourself nature), I went straight into my prayer room. Unfortunately, when you are in that state of mind (the flesh), it's easy to respond in a way that is not pleasing to God. That is not who I am anymore. I have chosen not to respond in a way that's not pleasing to our Father. I need the Holy Spirit to bury *Bo-Nita*, the flesh.

This is where we have to say to ourselves, as stated in Scripture, "He must increase, but I must decrease" (John 3:30, KJV). When we find ourselves in these situations, it's easy to fall into the pattern of our flesh, especially when a person or a situation has left a bad taste in our mouths. The familiar, unpleasant feeling is a trigger for us. In these moments, we need God to increase in us so we will decrease.

In order for Him to increase in me, I had to go into His presence and allow Him to calm me down and speak to me. Scripture states, "He that dwelleth in the secret place of the Most-High (EL Shaddai) shall abide under the shadow of the Almighty (El- Elyon)" (Psalm 91:1, KJV).

I learned I needed to be in His presence to calm down and hear His voice. I can't hear God's voice when I'm in a rage. If I can't hear God, I will react in an unseemly manner.

I was about to confront the matter, but the Holy Spirit led me to my prayer room. Once in my prayer room, I began to talk to the Lord. I reminded Him of the promises He personally gave me through His Word. Unfortunately, I was now seeing things manifested in my life that were drastically different from what I expected. "Lord, You told me, 'No weapon formed against me shall prosper'" (Isaiah 54:17, KJV). It looked as if the weapon was prospering. It appeared to me that one of the fiery darts had penetrated my shield and was stinging me. The enemy was pushing me to act out of character. *Bo-Nita* was in a rage!

In my anger, I was finally ready to go confront my husband about this situation. God allowed me to say everything I wanted to say. Then, at the end of my ranting and raving, the Lord said, "You will say nothing!" He said for me not to mention it to my husband. I sat down and said, "Lord! I'm not going to be able to say anything?" He responded by saying, "The only thing I want you to do is to love your husband. Love on your husband." Therefore, I sat down and cried. I knew God had spoken, and I knew that I had to be obedient.

This is how God usually cleanses us from bad aftertaste. He tells us to do nothing while He takes the lead. Bad taste usually leads to bad experiences when we do not allow Him preeminence.

This was a hard thing, but God's ways are not our ways. His ways are always better than ours as Isaiah 55:8-9 tells us. The Bible also states, "If we confess our sins, He's faithful and just to forgive us our sins and cleanse us from all unrighteousness" (1 John 1:9, KJV). At that time, I had to ask God to forgive me for my thoughts and what I wanted to do and say because I was angry.

Sometimes we go through things in life, and we get angry. These memories have left a bad taste in our mouths. I'm so grateful and thankful that God did not let me do anything stupid. We make mistakes when we're angry and operating in our flesh. When God speaks to us, we'd better listen. For everyone reading this book, God said to me, "You will say nothing! You will not even mention it to him."

Today, I can honestly say to you that I never mentioned this situation to my husband before he left this earth. I did exactly what the Lord told me to do. In my obedience, God blessed me. How did He bless me? He blessed me with peace and with a closer relationship with my husband and with Him.

Sometimes you need an outlet. You need a person to talk to and bounce things off. Imagine someone going through something that causes such hurt and anger and having no one to turn to. They suffer in silence and may become bitter and angry with God. When they look at their life, it doesn't add up, especially when they are reminded of the Word of God. God has made you some promises, and you feel His promises are not being fulfilled because of what you're going through.

When I think back on the situation, the only thing I can do is give God the glory for helping me keep my big mouth shut at a critical time in our lives. As bad a time as this was for us, I would have felt even worse had I not been obedient to God's instructions. I could have overridden what God said like I may do when I'm upset.

In all honesty, I don't always listen when I know God is speaking to me, especially when I'm angry. So often in anger, I am rarely quick to listen and slow to speak as we are instructed in James 1:19. Sometimes I feel I have to say something.

I thank God for my obedience. Because of this, God gave me peace that surpasses all understanding. The Lord loved the both of us. He didn't want me to have any regrets, and He didn't want my husband going through dealing with a cancer diagnosis alone and frustrated. He wanted him to know He had his back, and I would be right there with him through it all. God loved both of us too much to allow us to get it wrong in this critical hour.

In case you are wondering what this situation was between my husband and me, the Lord told me not to mention it to my husband, so I see no need in disclosing it to anyone else. I included this incident in the book because people face many challenges in relationships.

Everybody's relationship is different, and we all have diverse challenges. Things that make me angry or trigger me may not do the same for you. What's considered *a bad taste* for me might not be considered *a bad taste* for you. Some situations may appear to be unforgivable, but I encourage you to stop, pray, and listen to what the Holy Spirit is saying to you at that moment. Allow God to speak to your heart before you approach someone you are at odds with. Approaching someone in the wrong spirit could cause irreparable damage to that relationship.

Self-Reflection:

This is how God usually cleanses us from bad aftertaste. He tells us to do nothing while He takes the lead. Bad taste usually leads to bad experiences when we do not allow Him preeminence.

1. What in your past keeps you from moving forward?

_____
_____
_____
_____
_____
_____
_____
_____
_____
_____
_____
_____
_____
_____

2. What does the new you look like versus the old you?

3. What things do you need to change in your life to move forward?

DOES YOUR PALATE NEED CLEANSING?

4. What memories have left a *bad taste* and are keeping you from living in peace?

   _____
   _____
   _____
   _____
   _____
   _____
   _____
   _____

5. What do you think God is telling you to stop doing?

   _____
   _____
   _____
   _____
   _____
   _____
   _____
   _____
   _____
   _____
   _____

Scripture References:

John 3:30
Psalm 91:1
Isaiah 54:17
Isaiah 55:8-9
1 John 1:9
James 1:19
Philippians 4:6

CHAPTER 4

Sweet

Merriam-Webster Dictionary defines sweet as "being, inducing, or marked by the one of the five basic taste sensations that is usually pleasing to the taste and typically induced by sugars (as sucrose or glucose); Pleasing to the mind or feelings; agreeable, gratifying. Marked by gentle good humor or kindliness."

During Bobby's illness, I saw a side of him that I had very seldom seen. I still got on his nerves for not moving fast enough to do things for him or not cooking his food just right. However, I saw God changing him in how he cared for me as his wife. He did everything in his power to take care of me and prepare me for his death.

For example, on our way home after one of his treatments, he insisted on going shopping at BJ's, a local wholesale club. He was very weak, so he had to drive one of the motorized carts to get around in the store. He started on the first aisle and proceeded to go down every aisle! At one point we got to the baby food section, and I told him we should skip this section. He refused to listen! We stayed in that store for three hours. I still have aluminum foil, Ziploc bags and so much more from that trip to the store. Even when we are weary and in the wilderness, God can give you a sweet taste to encourage you. Sometimes it feels like He is slow to intervene, but the truth of the matter is that He is meticulous and strategic.

A couple of months before my husband passed, he asked Rob, our neighbor, to repair everything that needed repairing at our home. Rob was at our home almost daily working on the repairs. Even though he did not complete *his list* before my husband transitioned, I am so grateful to Rob and his entire family for all they did for me and my husband while he was living and for me after he passed.

Additionally, my neighbors, Lyle and Ms. Emma, Eric and Michelle, and Douglas were amazing. I can never thank them enough for the help they rendered. As I look back over this time in my life, it is comforting to see how Bobby made me a priority. He cared for me and our home at a time when he was experiencing pain and suffering.

Bobby and Bonita Womack

Self-Reflection:

If your heart is open, you can taste the sweet aroma even in your wilderness journey.

DOES YOUR PALATE NEED CLEANSING?

1. Are you missing the sweet aroma of your wilderness journey?

2. How can your taste affect your journey?

___

Scripture References:

Philippians 4:13
John 14:27

CHAPTER 5

Unsavory

Dictionary.com defines unsavory as not savory; tasteless or insipid; an unsavory meal, unpleasant in taste or smell; distasteful. Unappealing or disagreeable, as a pursuit.

One day after we left one of his radiation appointments, Bobby and I were discussing what they told him at the doctor's office concerning the radiation. The treatment was not working, and the tumors were still growing. It was during this conversation he realized he needed to make some preparations.

My husband contacted Bishop Dedric Hood and invited him into our home to discuss his final arrangements. Bishop Hood and First Lady Tachala Hood came over to visit a couple of weeks before he transitioned.

Frequently during my husband's last days, he would advise of his wishes and desires after death. He was very detailed. He gave me clear instructions on what he wanted the family to wear for his homegoing service. He told me what to say to the people at the service. He strongly encouraged me to take better care of myself.

Every time he thought about leaving me, he would be in tears. He said, "I'm leaving and who's going to take care of you, Bonita?" I said, "God has taken care of me to this point in my life and I know He will continue. Don't worry about me. We are all concerned about you. You are not leaving!" I kept telling him, "You're not leaving so stop saying that." He still struggled with me being left alone.

I've come to realize that my husband was heartbroken with the thought of leaving me and no longer being able to care for me. He often said God gave me to him, and it was his responsibility to care for me. God walked me through this time day by day.

As I walked through it, there were times I couldn't believe Bobby's strength. He had a lot of strength. When I tell you he fought, my husband fought. He said, "I'm fighting to the end," and he did! As I reflect and replay all that happened during that time, I realized he planned everything. If you knew my husband, Bobby Womack Sr., you know that he loved being in control and would always try to dominate everything.

I used to tell him that he was no longer in the military. He wasn't my sergeant, and he wasn't going to tell me what to do. I knew he was my husband, and I should have listened to him more. He was militant. He was rough. I believe I went through some things with him that the average wife probably will never go through, and some would not be able to handle or choose to handle.

During the rough times, I realized that God never left my side. He was teaching and preparing me to stand during this trial that we were going through. My husband was a different kind of man. Sometimes that difference got on my last nerve. I would often say, "Bobby didn't get on your last nerve, he got under your fingernails." I recall many times when people would say to me that he was a handful. I responded, "No, he's not a handful. You've got to put both hands up. You've got to juggle this joker; you can't handle him." He was *a whole lot!* When I think about it now, I laugh at some of the things I experienced. I learned so much from him. God also taught me a great deal through this marriage. Regardless of the trials and tribulations we experienced, it was an amazing journey that I will never forget. I can say a lot of things about my husband. If he was here, he would have a lot to say about me as well.

I am not perfect by a long stretch, and we didn't have a perfect marriage. God knows we didn't. As I talk about Bobby, please understand I am not portraying I am perfect by any means; hence, the need for palate cleansing. We both were broken people who needed God's healing.

After my husband's death, the Lord revealed I had some lingering aftertastes from past relationships and pain from the past. I saw what my husband went through, and it was painful for me to watch. It was painful for me to see him wither from the big-framed man to the shell of a man he was when he left this earth. Because of what I saw my husband go through, God knew I needed cleansing and healing.

Watching someone go through the death journey is hard and painful. Many times, it leaves you broken, even if your faith is strong. It can leave an unsavory aftertaste. I saw Bobby walk through his sickness, fighting all the way.

One day, near the end of his battle, he fell and I was not able to help him up. I called his brothers, my best friend, and her husband to come over to help. Once they arrived, they were able to lift him from the floor back to the bed. After we got him settled, my husband asked everyone to come around the bed. He proceeded to give everyone instructions. He asked all of them to look out for me and to make sure I would be okay. He also gave words to them as well.

So much of his suffering was engraved in my brain. It kept playing repeatedly in my mind, the lingering aftertaste. As a result, I took advantage of the professional counseling services offered to me through hospice and The Employee Assistance Program (EAP). I encourage you to do the same if you need someone to talk to concerning issues that affect your well-being. Please do not suffer in silence!

Self-Reflection:

1. What painful unsavory aftertaste are you harboring?

2. Have you considered professional counseling? If so, what was that experience like?

3. If you feel you need help, what is holding you back?

___

Scripture References:

Hebrews 11:6, 12:1
Proverbs 16:3

CHAPTER 6

Salty

According to Urbandictionary.com, salty is described as "the combination of being both sour and bitter."

Before my husband got sick, he was a big man, and I was a big girl. We had a queen-sized bed, and I would always say to him, "Why are you on my side of the bed?" We would argue about this often. I would say," Bobby, you're not giving me any room, and I have hot flashes." I'm sure many of you ladies know exactly what I mean! When you're having hot flashes, it feels as if you are going to ignite! I would tell my husband all the time, "Get on your side!" He would say, "You ain't got no side!" I would then reply, "You have to move over." Each time I would try to turn over in bed, he would be under me, and I would say, "Oh my goodness. I am going to die in this bed if I don't get some room to breathe."

As my husband went through his sickness, I saw him get smaller and smaller in bed. One night, I reached over to the right to touch him, and I didn't feel him in the bed. I thought he had gotten up. Then, I looked over, and he was at the edge of the bed on the other side. My arm did not reach him because he was just that thin. Seeing my husband, whom I loved dearly, suffer from cancer was heartbreaking.

I encourage the husbands and wives reading this book not to waste opportunities to embrace and enjoy each other. Time is something you can't get back. When it's gone, it's gone. Don't let petty stuff like fussing or disagreeing create division in your relationships. This saltiness of divisiveness and disunity leads to a bitter palate.

My husband and I went through a lot of things in our marriage and had many challenges. I realize things could have been different if we allowed God to do the necessary palate cleansing. I encourage you to take inventory of your marriage and begin to see those things you need God to cleanse from your palate. Take inventory of why you do the things you do or don't do. Is there residue from past relationships? Is there residue from past hurt and pain? Is there residue from things that you and your spouse went through or are still going through? God is ready to mend all the broken places in your relationships.

Are you moving forward? Are you stuck by the salty aftertaste? The salty residue can be compounded from experiences with not only your spouse but with family members, friends, co-workers, church members, children, parents, and even unresolved issues from your childhood.

I really hope by reading this you can see things in a different light. We are all a work in progress. Whether you've been in your marriage one month, six months, 20 years, or 30 years or more, I'm sure it's something you can learn from this book that can make an immediate difference in your marriage. By making small changes and taking inventory of our behavior, we can improve our marriage. It really can be the little things that make the biggest difference.

Is there something that you need to address right now? Maybe you need to reach out to a counselor. Just take inventory of your life and ask God for guidance. Don't go out in public and act one way and go home and be totally different. Hurt people hurt people! It's no need to walk around with a salty palate if your palate can be cleansed by God. David said in (Psalm 51:10), "Create in me a clean heart, O God; and renew a right spirit within me." Ask Him to create in you a clean heart and renew the right spirit within you so you can operate in that place in the right spirit and not based on your pain.

At this time, I thank God that He's showing me the mistakes I've made. I know if my husband was here today, he would be so happy to hear that God revealed this to me. I can hear him saying, "Hallelujah, hallelujah, hallelujah!" Even though it's after the fact, I'm excited I recognized there were things I didn't do right and could have done better. If my palate wasn't so salty, I might have understood my husband a lot better. Because of my salty palate, I'm sure I blocked many blessings. But now, thanks be to God, I am open to hearing and doing what God says to me like never before.

According to Apostle James W. Willie III, Pastor of Obedience to the Word Church, "Divine intervention is needed to get yourself together. You can't get yourself together by yourself. God called us out of darkness into His marvelous light. He didn't call us out of light, but He called us out of darkness." Apostle Willie added that all of us were in darkness, and all of us came out with some residue of the darkness. There are three persons who will have to be addressed to understand where you are as you measure your walk with the Lord. Your old you, your now you, and your becoming you. He went on to say, "There is the old you, if you are saved."

Again, that's with the assumption that you are born again. If you are not saved, the old you is still the new you and the becoming you. (2 Cor 5:17, KJV) states, "Therefore if any man be in Christ, he is a new creature: old things are passed away; behold, all things are become new."

Apostle Willie went on to say, "When you are in Christ, you are new in spirit, but you still have old memories, old issues, and old residue that you always will be contending with. The darkness that you were in will determine the level of aggressiveness you will need to be in the presence of the Lord. Even though we were all born in sin, some of us went through some very destructive things. We need to renew our minds constantly."

We should hide the Scripture in our hearts. Our continuous plea should be for God to create a clean heart and renew a right spirit within us.

Self-Reflection:

Don't let petty stuff like fussing or disagreeing create division in your relationships. This saltiness of divisiveness and disunity leads to a bitter palate.

1. What has your palate salty?

_____

_____

_____

_____

_____

_____

_____

_____

_____

_____

_____

_____

_____

_____

2. What is your greatest regret?

3. What would you like to see changed in your life?

___

Scripture References:

2 Cor. 5:17
Psalm 51:10

CHAPTER 7

Distasteful

According to Oxford Languages Dictionary, distasteful is "causing dislike or disgust; offensive; unpleasant; Even anger can be considered distasteful."

Anger has been referred to as an emotion that can wreak havoc in our lives when not properly channeled. Anger is defined as "a strong feeling of annoyance, displeasure or hostility." When you are angry, it's easy to see yourself as a victim. Once you are in this state of mind, it's like having on blinders. Unfortunately, it's hard to see anything else.

There were many times in my life when I saw myself as a victim. When you see yourself as a victim, your reality is distorted. Unless God changes your mindset, it can be extremely challenging to get past this place of feeling you have been wronged. It is so easy to focus on the negative and exaggerate the bad things happening to us. Until we stop seeing ourselves as the victim or adopting the victim's mentality, we won't be able to see that sometimes we contribute to our own issues. We may focus only on the other person and the part they play. We remain in this state until we recognize we may need help and allow God to minister to us about the various issues in our lives. We may also continue to experience feelings that are distasteful.

When we hear from God, we can operate differently. We can then see that we give others control when we operate with a victim's mentality. In his article, "Beware of The Dangers of a Victim Mentality," 12/8/2020, thegospelcoalition.org, Akos Balogh advises, "The victim mentality magnifies the harm done to us, and minimizes our own sinfulness. After all, we reason our sin is nothing compared to what others have done to us. Except for circumstances where we are innocent victims (e.g. when robbed at gunpoint etc.), we often have some responsibility for our situation. We often have some part to play in the way things have turned out (even if only partially). But a victim mentality tells a false narrative, explaining our situation so that blame lies exclusively with other people/circumstances."

Balogh further points out that victim mentality "disempowers us, sucks the joy out of life and damages relationships." He suggests a better way is to entrust your life to God while doing good. "A victim mentality is not a biblical response to unjust suffering."

Apostle Peter states, "This is the kind of life you've been invited into, the kind of life Christ lived. He suffered everything that came his way so you would know that it could be done, and know how to do it, step-by-step. He never did one thing wrong, not once said anything amiss. They called him every name in the book, and he said nothing back. He suffered in silence, content to let God set things right. He used his servant body to carry our sins to the cross so we could be rid of sin, free to live the right way. His wounds became your healing. You were lost sheep with no idea who you were or where you were going. Now you're named and kept for good by the Shepherd of your souls" (1 Peter 2:21-25).

Praise the Lord! When we look at all God has done for us, how can we have a spirit of unforgiveness? So many times, unforgiveness develops as a result of anger, hostility, misunderstanding, victimization, hurt, and pain.

The Apostle Peter asks Jesus how many times one forgives someone who sins against you. Jesus answers seventy-seven times. Forgiving someone seventy-seven times in one day is not our reality. We find ourselves holding a grudge and not being able to forgive. Time and time again, we ask God for forgiveness for our sins, but we are unable to forgive those who sinned against us.

Refusing to forgive can result in a closed-off heart. Unforgiveness is sinful and is distasteful. It can negatively affect our lives in so many ways. If not dealt with, it can cause a root of bitterness that can grow and take over a person's life. As previously noted, unforgiveness chains you and does not allow you to heal, which in turn can cause sickness and even death. Forgiveness is the only way to cleanse the distaste from our palate.

Furthermore, unforgiveness is an open door for Satan to come in to distract, deceive, and destroy. The Bible talks a lot about unforgiveness and bitterness being a problem. Scripture states, "See to it that no one falls short of God's grace; that no root of resentment springs up and causes trouble, and by it, many are defiled" (Hebrews 12:15, NIV).

As I think about all of this, I thank God that unforgiveness no longer has a root in my life. Because of God's grace and mercy, I am no longer bound by anger and bitterness. This was not an overnight fix. Over the years, God has continuously worked in my life as I experienced different things. I can recall how I handled things as a teenager and a young adult. I would do things differently today. Life's experiences have taught me that nothing is wasted.

Self-Reflection:

Refusing to forgive can result in a closed-off heart. Unforgiveness is sinful and is distasteful. Forgiveness is the only way to cleanse the distaste from our palate.

1. Who are you really?

   _____
   _____
   _____
   _____
   _____
   _____
   _____
   _____
   _____
   _____
   _____
   _____
   _____
   _____
   _____

2. How do you cope with life's challenges?

   _____
   _____
   _____
   _____

DOES YOUR PALATE NEED CLEANSING?

3. Are you holding on to something you need to let go of?

4. Do you consider yourself a victim? Why or why not?

Scripture References:

1 Peter 2:21-25
Hebrews 12:15
Matthew 18

CHAPTER 8

Unappetizing

Dictionary.com defines unappetizing as an adjective "(of food) not pleasing or stimulating to the appetite (of prospect, person, etc.) not appealing or attractive or pleasant."

Everything we go through in life has a purpose. When we think of the pandemic, most of us automatically think it was a terrible, devastating situation. Indeed, it was! However, when I look back and see how some things played out during this time, I can see the hand of God was at work.

It was during the time of the pandemic that Bobby and I went through his sickness. At the beginning of the pandemic, we had no idea what was ahead. Thankfully, God allowed me to work from home, and I was able to spend time with him during his battle with cancer. We got to interact and talk a lot more during this time.

The pandemic revealed a lot of things that were under the surface and some of those things were very unappetizing. These are experiences wherein we feel stuck, closed in and not knowing how to escape. I witnessed marriages failing, families falling apart, and children experiencing all kinds of emotional challenges.

According to healthychildren.org, in December 2021, "The ongoing stress, fear, grief, and uncertainty created by COVID-19 pandemic has weighed heavily on children and teens. Many are having a tough time coping emotionally. More than 140,000 children in the United States have experienced the death of a parent or grandparent caregiver from COVID." On the other hand, some families got to spend a lot more quality time together and their bonds were strengthened. We are all now attempting to adjust to our new normal.

My job was very gracious to me and allowed me to make up hours if needed. My manager was very flexible, and I thank God for that. Being at home afforded me the opportunity to see things a lot differently. Many times, I looked for reasons to get out of the house to escape what was going on at home. As I said before, we don't always get it right. Caregiving can be an extremely difficult task, and it is so unappetizing. It is very important that those caring for others make time to care for themselves. It was comforting to get out of the environment at home, even if just for a moment. The way to cleanse your palate in this situation is a break from the ordinary and getting around other positive people.

Opportunities to attend worship services were a welcomed break. It was uplifting to spend time with brothers and sisters in Christ and to worship with them. Scripture states, "Not giving up meeting together, as some are in the habit of doing, but encouraging one another—and all the more as you see the Day approaching" (Hebrews 10:25 NIV).

When you are experiencing unappetizing events, it is important to fellowship with other believers. Scripture tells us to encourage one another. Thankfully, there were family members who came to my aid anytime I left home. They were truly a blessing to us. Quite frankly, I don't know how I would have made it without them. We were encouraged in word and deed.

Even though there were many times that our family and friends came to our aid, still there were times when we had to face issues head-on and alone. During the pandemic shutdown, we didn't go places unless we had to. We were more or less locked in.

Surprisingly, this reminded me of times the prayer ministry held shut-ins at my home. For three days we fasted and prayed for various things going on in our lives and in the body of Christ. What an analogy! Maybe this is what we need today. We need a shut-in right now. We need to turn our faces to Christ Jesus and allow Him to minister to each of us in our respective relationships.

I'm not only talking about husbands and wives, but this goes for parents with children, sisters and brothers, teachers and students and relationships among friends. We need to stop running from whatever the situation is and deal with it. Resolution should be the goal.

Don't wait for God to allow a personal shutdown, where we can't go anywhere. With His help, we can do this. Stop right now and ask God for His guidance. I suggest that you stop right here, fold the page over in the book, and come back later.

Spend some time with God and see if He directs you to address whatever issues you may be facing. In facing your issues or your *giants*, you may save yourself or others with whom you have relationships from unnecessary hurt and pain.

We know the pandemic brought a lot of death. It brought a lot of bad things to a lot of people. We are still suffering through this pandemic right now as I write this book. I lost several family members during the pandemic. Despite all the losses, we experienced some good during this time, even if we didn't always see it.

I now see how God carried me through. He subtly revealed things to me about myself and gave me peace even though I was in the midst of a storm.

He allowed us to have time to be in the house together to talk things through. My husband used this time to prepare me for his transition. God allowed us both to see life through a bigger frame.

Self-Reflection:

When you are experiencing unappetizing events, it is important to fellowship with other believers. Spending time with others can be a positive distraction.

1. Do you feel stuck or closed in? If so, what is your escape route?

_____
_____
_____
_____
_____
_____
_____
_____
_____
_____
_____
_____
_____
_____
_____
_____
_____
_____

DOES YOUR PALATE NEED CLEANSING?

Scripture References:

1 Corinthians 10:13
Hebrews 10:25

CHAPTER 9

Refreshment

Oxford Languages Dictionary defines refreshment as, "the giving of fresh mental or physical strength or energy."

In 2021, I ran into Felicia Lucas, whom I originally met a couple years earlier at a women's event. When I met Felicia, there was something about her that drew me to her. I talked with her for a few moments after the event was over, and we later connected on Messenger.

I walked into a local establishment to make a purchase and saw Felicia, though I barely recognized her. I said, "Is your name Felicia, Felicia Lucas?" She said, "Yes." I was amazed at what I saw! She was totally different from the woman I met in 2019, and it was not just because she was smaller in size.

I could sense there was something totally different about her. What I saw was a woman who reminded me of (Hebrews 12:1, KJV Bible) which states, "Wherefore seeing we also are compassed about with so great a cloud of witnesses, let us lay aside every weight, and the sin which doth so easily beset us, and let us run with patience the race that is set before us." She appeared to not be weighted down with "stuff." She looked so relaxed, calm, and at peace. Ironically, we were at a massage parlor where she was waiting to get a massage.

What I saw in the spirit was a cleansed palate! I knew right then and there what God wanted to do in my life. I immediately asked her to give me a business card and told her I would be in touch. I reached out to Felicia in June of 2021. She explained her journey concerning the changes in her life and informed me that she was a health coach.

This is where my journey began. It was ironic that I would run into Felicia a few days before I was scheduled to deliver a message speaking on the *palate*. God's provision and timing are always perfect. When He speaks to you and you listen and are obedient, He will show you exactly what you need. He will sometimes put the people in front of you to help you navigate your way through your new journey.

With the help of the Lord, Felicia assisted me to get to the place I am today. A refreshing change took place in my life. I began to *taste* and *see* life differently. I am a different person, a much lighter person. I'm doing some things I thought I would never do. For example, I am going back to school, starting a business, eating healthier, growing a garden, developing a love for music that soothes the soul, and writing a book.

After four months of being on the Optimal Weight 5 & 1 Plan with Optavia, I decided to start training to become an Optavia coach. I started the program and learned the necessary steps to become a coach. It was evident to me that the program worked. There was a difference in my physical, spiritual, and mental health. I applied to take the required examination to become an Independent Certified Optavia Coach. Thankfully, I passed the exam.

Over the course of eight months on this program, I was able to lose 100 pounds.

"Average Weight loss on the Optimal Weight 5 & 1 plan is 12 pounds. Clients are in weight loss, on average, for 12 weeks."

Even though I gained a few pounds back in the last year, I am in a much healthier place in my life. Losing weight has helped to lower my blood pressure. Because of my lifestyle change, I am much healthier, mentally and physically. This required a change of wardrobe. I was able to give several of my clothes to charitable donations, family, and friends. I stepped into a new makeover. God gave me a makeover, not only in outward appearance but in my heart, mind, spirit, and soul.

My mom would be so proud to know that I could fit into her dress.

Changing my lifestyle enabled me to start a business as a coach. **Please reach out to me at https://believingforbetterwithbonita.com and allow me to walk with you on your new journey.**

Although I saw this as a ministry, I have been able to increase my household income. With that being said, I went from being a coach to being an executive director in one year. However, like any business, you have your ups and downs, but I will not give up on what God started in my life. Please reach out and allow me to walk with you on your new journey.

Since this change in my life, God has allowed me to coach several beautiful women into a new and refreshing place in their lives. I have applied my *cleansing the palate detailing* as a part of my training. I am seeing remarkable results from women on every level (pastors, ministers, housewives, friends, family, etc.), as they too are experiencing a new beginning as I have.

I thank God for the beautiful refreshing experiences encountered during these coaching opportunities. "I can do all things through him who strengthens me" (Philippians 4:13).

Felicia has been an integral part of my "weight loss" journey. However, God revealed so much more during this process. In all honesty, weight loss was my primary focus, but God quickly diverted my focus to other areas of my life. I'm so thankful to Felicia for her example and for her showing me how it's done. I give God strong glory for her. She has helped me tremendously. God knows how to *hook a sistah up*, and I thank Him for placing Felicia in my life.

Additionally, I also began an exercise program. My chiropractor, John Lancaster of Cary Chiropractic Partners, once told me of a quote he read, "Exercise is not a punishment for the things you eat. It's a celebration of the things your body can do." He went on to say, "The best position is your next position. Movement is the key to life so keep moving."

Another medium I now use to cleanse my palate is music. The ministry of music can soothe your soul, quiet your spirit, and take you into the presence of the Lord.

I urge you to be careful not to go back to the place from which you have been delivered. In life, you will be thrown curve balls. As I look back over my life, I realize I have experienced many obstacles.

I know it's not over. Throughout this journey called life, God has kept me and allowed me not to give up on myself. 1 Peter 5:7 reminds us to cast all our worries and cares on Him for He cares about what happens to us. God gave me a word. He spoke one word to me, and it changed the trajectory of my life.

What is your one word? What is God saying to you? I encourage you to stop and allow God to minister to you concerning the areas He reveals to you. Only God can mend and heal a broken heart. It doesn't matter how the brokenness occurred, or how long it's been there. God is able to remove every single lingering aftertaste and completely abolish the residue from any and everything you have experienced. Again, cast your cares on God, and trust Him fully with your life. This is not the end of our story. It's only the beginning. Praise God!

Self-Reflection:

Throughout this journey called life, God has kept me and allowed me not to give up on myself. Don't give up! God is not through with you.

1. Who are the people that inspire you?

   _____

   _____

   _____

   _____

   _____

   _____

   _____

2. What is the ideal version of yourself?

   _____

   _____

   _____

   _____

   _____

3. What are your passions?

Scripture References:

Hebrews 12:1
Philippians 4:13
1 Peter 5:7

CHAPTER 10

Leftovers for Your Takeout

It has taken almost two years to get where I am today. During the palate cleansing process, I had tremendous losses in my life. I lost three siblings, several family members, and recently a dear friend who was as close as a sister to me. Also, several of my friends experienced losses that affected me because of the close relationship I have with them.

You can have the same or similar situations going on in your life to cause you to pause the work that God is doing to cleanse your palate. I realize that palate cleansing is an ongoing journey. Things may happen along the way that could cause a build-up of residue on your palate. We must stay encouraged, stay focused, and remain open to the cleansing process. God will finish what He started!

Taste and See

I would like to invite you to surrender your heart to Jesus. The Word of God states, "Look! I have been standing at the door, and I am constantly knocking. If anyone hears me calling him and opens the door, I will come in and fellowship with him, and he with me" (Revelation 3:20, TLB).

If you feel the Lord knocking on the door of your heart right now, I encourage you to let Him in. Don't miss this opportunity. God is drawing you to Himself. As noted in Scripture, "If you declare with your mouth, 'Jesus is Lord,' and believe in your heart that God raised him from the dead, you will be saved. For it is with your heart that you believe and are justified, and it is with your mouth that you profess your faith and are saved" (Romans 10:9-10, NIV Bible).

Simply pray the following prayer:

> *Lord, I know I'm a sinner. Forgive me for all my sins. I ask you to come into my heart and cleanse me of all unrighteousness. I believe Jesus died on the cross for my sins, and you raised Him from the dead just for me. Lord, thank you for saving me. I pray this in Jesus' name. Amen.*

Maybe you are reading this book and are saved and out of fellowship with God. He is calling you back to Himself. He's standing with open arms ready to receive you. Ask Him for forgiveness and pray the following prayer:

> *Lord, I admit that I sinned against you and need your forgiveness. Forgive me of all my sins, come into my heart and make me whole again. Thank You, Lord, for forgiving me. In Jesus' name. Amen.*

About the Author

Bonita Williams Womack is an ordained evangelist and church elder. Bonita resides in Willow Spring, NC. She has ministered the gospel in foreign missions in Guayaquil, Ecuador.

She is a noted teacher and trainer in the field of evangelism. Her desire is that she continuously and completely yields to the power of the Holy Spirit and that the ministry of reconciliation be manifested in her life as well as others.

She has studied management from the University of Notre Dame and is pursuing an associate degree in accounting from Liberty University in Lynchburg, VA.

Elder Womack strives to live a holistic lifestyle and is an Independent Certified Optavia Coach.

The following books are a few suggested inspirational reads. They are available on Amazon.

An Invitation to the Extraordinary by Phillip A. Walker

The Reinvention of Me by Felicia C. Lucas

Deliverance for Real by Dr. Shirley R. Brown Th.D

What's going on with Mommy? by Monisha Parker

Self Exam by Monisha Parker and Sylvia Morrison can be ordered at https://purposepaintedpink.com/selfexam

His Glory Creations Publishing, LLC is an International Christian Book Publishing Company, established in 2017, which helps launch the creative fiction and non-fiction works of new, aspiring, and seasoned authors across the globe, through stories that are inspirational, empowering, life changing or educational in nature, including anthologies, poetry, journals, children's books, and recipe books.

DESIRE TO KNOW MORE?

Contact Information:
CEO/Founder: Felicia C. Lucas
www.hisglorycreationspublishing.com
Email: hgcpublishingllc@gmail.com
Office Phone: 919-679-1706
Facebook: His Glory Creations Publishing
Instagram: His Glory Creations Publishing
YouTube: His Glory Creations Publishing

Made in the USA
Columbia, SC
21 November 2024